The Kingdom Builder Paul's Bold Proclamation of Christ

Joshua Rhoades

Published by Joshua Paul Rhoades, 2024.

While every precaution has been taken in the preparation of this book, the publisher assumes no responsibility for errors or omissions, or for damages resulting from the use of the information contained herein.

THE KINGDOM BUILDER PAUL'S BOLD PROCLAMATION OF CHRIST

First edition. October 13, 2024.

Copyright © 2024 Joshua Rhoades.

ISBN: 979-8227455543

Written by Joshua Rhoades.

Also by Joshua Rhoades

Courage Under Fire: David's Stand On The Battlefield
Jonah's Journey: Voices Of Redemption And Lessons In Obedience
The Furnace Of Faith: 12 Principles From The Heat Of Faith
Whispers of Hope: Inspiring Stories of Men's Prayers In Scripture
Frontier Legends: The Oregon Dream
Elijah: A Beacon Of Boldness
HOOK, LINE & SAVIOUR - Faith Reflections from Fishing
Driven By Faith: Motor Racing Inspired Christian Life
30 Day Devotional - Bold and Strong- Coffee Devotions for a Courageous
Christian Walk
Authentic Christianity: The Heart of Old Time Religion
Consider The Ant - God's Tiny Preachers
Flee Fornication: The Plea For Purity
Renewed Hope- How to Find Encouragement in God
Sounding The Call - The Voice of Conviction
The Altar - Where Heaven Meets Earth
The Bible's Battlefields- Timeless Lessons from Ancient Wars
The Sacred Art of Silence - How Silence Speaks in Scripture
Under Fire- The Sanctity of the Traditional Biblical Home
Who Is on the Lord's Side? A Call to Righteousness
What Is Truth? - From Skepticism to Submission
First and Goal- Faith and Football Fundamentals
From Dugout to Devotion- Spiritual Lessons from Baseball
Par for the Course- Faith and Fairways
The Believer's Pace- Tools for Running Life's Marathon
The Immutable Fortress- Security in God's Unchanging Nature
Biblical Bravery
Deer Stands and Devotions: A Hunter's Walk with God

Jesus Knows- Our Hearts, Our Responsibility
Restoration - Setting The Bone
Spiritual 911- God's Word for Life's Emergency's
The Freedom of Forgiveness
The Jezebel Effect - Ancient Manipulations Modern Lessons
The Shout That Stopped The Saviour
The Time Machine Chronicles: Old Testament Characters
Anchored In Truth Exploring The Depths of Psalm 119
Biblical Counsel on Anger
Proverbs' Portraits The Men God Mentions
Stumbling in the Dark - The Dangers of Alcohol
Guarding the Wicket Protecting Your Faith and Game
The Champion's Faith - Wrestling and Achieving Spiritual Victory
Scriptural Commands for Modern Times Living God's Word Today Volume 1
Scriptural Commands for Modern Times Living God's Word Today Volume 2
Scriptural Commands for Modern Times Living God's Word TodayVolume3
The Greatest Gift
A Christmas Journey of Faith
Daughter Of The King: Embracing Your Identity In Christ
Determination and Dedication Building Strong Faith As A Young Man
Walking Through Walls God's Power to Part the Storms of Life
David's Song Of Deliverance Praising God Through Every Storm
From Weakness to Warrior: Gideon's Transformation
Why Did Jesus Weep?
Living For God The Call To Be A Living Sacrifice
My Mind Is In A Fog What Do I Do?
Turning The Page Written By Grace
The Calling and Greatness of John the Baptist
For Such a Time Esther's Courageous Stand
From Brokenness To Beauty Written By The Pen of Grace
The Ultimate Guide to Massive Action- From Plans to Reality
A Heart Of Conviction
Serving In The Shadows
Repentance Revealed The Road Back To God
The Chief Sinner Meets The Chief Saviour Reflections On I Timothy 1:15

Answer The Call - 31 Days of Biblical Action
The Birthmark of the Believer
Reflections on Calvary's Cross
The Kingdom Builder Paul's Bold Proclamation of Christ

Dedication

This book, "The Kingdom Builder: Paul's Bold Proclamation of Christ," is dedicated to you, the reader, who may be seeking encouragement, hope, or a deeper understanding of your faith journey. Whether you're facing trials, questioning your purpose, or longing for a sense of direction, know that just as God worked through the life of Paul, He is working in your life too. Paul, once a man who persecuted Christians, was radically transformed by an encounter with Jesus and became one of the boldest proclaimers of Christ's message. His story shows us that no one is too far from God's grace, and no past mistakes are too big for God to redeem. You may be walking through a season of struggle, feeling inadequate, or unsure of your purpose, but this book is here to remind you that God can use anyone—no matter where they've been—to do great things for His kingdom. Paul's life is a powerful example of how God calls imperfect people, strengthens them, and leads them to fulfill His purpose. Let Paul's unwavering faith, boldness, and courage inspire you to trust in God's plan for your life. The same power that transformed Paul is at work in you. You are capable of more than you realize because Christ's strength is made perfect in your weakness. You don't need to be perfect or have everything figured out. Like Paul, your journey is about trusting God and stepping forward in faith, even when you don't know what lies ahead. The Kingdom of God isn't built by those who are flawless, but by those who are willing to be used by God. As you read this book and reflect on Paul's incredible story, may you be reminded that God sees you, knows you, and has a purpose for your life that is bigger than you can imagine. He is calling you to boldly proclaim His love, just as Paul did. You may not feel like a kingdom builder right now, but with God's grace, you can be. This book is a reminder that God often chooses the unlikely, the broken, and the humble to accomplish His greatest works. Paul's story is filled with moments of triumph, hardship, and perseverance, and it serves as a beacon of hope for all of us who struggle along the way. If you're in a place where you're questioning whether God can use you, let this book encourage you to keep pressing on. The same God who strengthened Paul in his trials is with you now, equipping you to face whatever challenges lie ahead. Let Paul's boldness inspire you to be courageous in your faith, knowing that God can work through you in ways you never expected. So, to you—the reader, the seeker, the believer—this book is dedicated as a source of encouragement, hope, and faith. May it remind you that you are part of God's story, and He is building His kingdom through you, just as He did through Paul. Be bold, be brave, and trust that God's purpose for your life is far greater than you can imagine.

Introduction

In the book "The Kingdom Builder: Paul's Bold Proclamation of Christ," we embark on an inspiring journey through the life of one of the most courageous and influential figures in Christian history—the apostle Paul. Once a fierce persecutor of Christians, Paul experienced a life-altering encounter with Jesus Christ that transformed him into one of the gospel's most passionate and fearless messengers. His story is one of boldness, faith, perseverance, and relentless dedication to spreading the message of salvation through Christ, regardless of the cost. From the moment Paul's life was turned upside down on the road to Damascus, he embraced his new calling with a fiery determination to proclaim Christ to the world. What makes Paul's journey so compelling is the magnitude of the change he experienced and his unshakable commitment to his mission. Throughout his ministry, Paul faced incredible obstacles—imprisonment, beatings, shipwrecks, rejection, and even the constant threat of death—yet he never wavered in his dedication to proclaiming the name of Jesus. He was a man who understood the power and urgency of the gospel, and his life was a reflection of the belief that the message of Jesus was worth any sacrifice.

Paul's boldness was not just a character trait but a reflection of his deep faith in Christ. He understood that Jesus was the promised Messiah, the Son of God who had come to offer salvation to all people. This understanding fueled his passion and gave him the courage to preach in synagogues, public squares, homes, and even before kings. Paul didn't just proclaim Christ to those familiar with the message; he sought out new places and people who had never heard of Jesus. He was a pioneer, constantly pushing the boundaries of where the gospel had been preached, and he was willing to face any opposition to spread the message of salvation. Paul's life shows us what it looks like to live with unwavering confidence in the truth of the gospel, and his example challenges us to consider how we, too, can be bold in our faith and proclamation of Christ.

But Paul's story isn't just about boldness in the face of opposition; it's also about faithfulness. From the moment he encountered Christ, Paul's life was marked by a deep, enduring commitment to his mission. He didn't just start strong; he finished strong. Even in his final days, under house arrest in Rome, Paul continued to preach the gospel with boldness and confidence. His ministry didn't fade as he grew older or the challenges increased—if anything, his passion for Christ only deepened. Paul's faithfulness to the gospel, no matter the cost, is a powerful reminder that the Christian life is a marathon, not a sprint. It's not just about how we begin our journey with Christ—it's about staying faithful to the end, trusting that God will give us the strength to endure every challenge we face.

As we look into Paul's story in "The Kingdom Builder - Paul's Bold Proclamation of Christ," we will explore the many dimensions of his bold and faithful ministry. From his early days of preaching in Damascus to his missionary journeys across the Roman Empire and even to his final days in chains, Paul's life is a testament to the power of a life fully surrendered to Christ. His story is not just a historical account—it's a source of inspiration and challenge for every believer. We will see how Paul's unwavering commitment to preaching Christ, willingness to suffer for the gospel, and boldness in the face of danger can inspire us to live with the same passion and dedication to Christ.

Paul's journey reminds us that we are all called to be kingdom builders. Just as Paul dedicated his life to expanding the Kingdom of God by sharing Jesus's message, we are also invited to participate in this great mission. The gospel is still the most powerful message the world has ever known, and we, like Paul, have the privilege of sharing it with those who have never heard it. As we study Paul's life, we will be encouraged to step out in faith, speak boldly about Jesus, and remain faithful to our calling, knowing that our efforts, like Paul's, will have an eternal impact. Whether we are called to preach to large crowds, to share Christ in our everyday conversations, or to support the work of the gospel in other ways, we can look to Paul's example of faithfulness and boldness as we seek to fulfill our role in building the Kingdom of God.

Chapter 1 – Purposeful

From encountering Jesus on the road to Damascus, Paul was consumed with a singular, burning purpose. His life was transformed in an instant, and the persecutor of Christians became their most passionate advocate. Without hesitation, Paul immediately began to proclaim Christ in the synagogues, boldly declaring that Jesus is the Son of God. This was not a small or easy task. Paul knew the risks he faced, as he had once been among those who sought to silence the followers of Jesus. Yet, his newfound faith in Christ gave him an unshakable purpose, a mission clearer than anything he had ever experienced.

Paul's mission was straightforward: he lived to share the truth about Jesus. There was no confusion or doubt about what he was meant to do. He preached in the synagogues, the very places where Jewish leaders gathered, and told them that the Messiah they had long awaited was Jesus, the very one they had rejected. His message was simple but profound. Jesus is the Son of God, the Savior who had come to bring redemption to all people. This truth became the foundation of Paul's life and ministry. It was the message he would carry wherever he went, from city to city, through trials, imprisonment, and persecution. Nothing could deter him because his purpose was too great, too vital to be silenced.

Paul's transformation is one of the most potent examples of what it means to live with purpose. His entire life shifted from one of destruction to one of building—building the Kingdom of God. He didn't waste time worrying about what others would think or how dangerous his mission would be. Instead, he threw himself entirely into his calling, understanding that the message of Christ was far more important than his comfort or safety. The urgency with which Paul preached shows how deeply he believed in the truth he was proclaiming. He wasn't preaching for personal gain or recognition; he was driven by a desire to see people come to know Jesus and receive the gift of salvation. His life was no longer his own; it belonged to Christ and the mission of expanding God's Kingdom.

In Acts 9:20, it says that Paul "straightway" preached Christ in the synagogues, proclaiming that He is the Son of God. This shows that Paul didn't wait to become a seasoned preacher or to gather more knowledge before starting his ministry. He knew the most important thing he could do was start sharing the truth about Jesus immediately. His message was centered on the core truth of the gospel: Jesus is the Son of God, and He came to save us. This simplicity and clarity in Paul's purpose is something we can all learn from. We, too, are called to share the truth of Christ with the world. We don't have to wait until we feel entirely prepared or qualified. Like Paul, we must be willing to step out in faith and declare the truth of who Jesus is, trusting that God will use us for His glory.

Paul's boldness is inspiring. He spoke confidently and confidently, even when it put him in danger. He wasn't afraid of the consequences because he knew that the message of Christ was worth any cost. He faced opposition, ridicule, and threats to his life, but none of that could stop him. These challenges only seemed to strengthen his resolve. The more he preached, the more he grew in strength, both physically and spiritually. Acts 9:22 tells us that Paul "increased the more in strength, and confounded the Jews which dwelt at Damascus, proving that this is very Christ." Paul didn't just proclaim Jesus; he proved through Scripture and reason that Jesus was the Messiah. His deep understanding of the Scriptures and his personal experience of Christ made his testimony undeniable. Those who heard him could not argue against the truth he shared.

As believers today, we can take great encouragement from Paul's example. His life teaches us that when we live with a clear purpose—to share the truth of Christ—we can face any challenge with boldness. Our mission, like Paul's, is to make Christ known. Paul's determination reminds us that sharing the gospel is not always easy, but it is always worth it. The message of salvation is the most important message anyone can hear, and we are called to be the ones to share it.

Paul's story also shows us the power of a life transformed by Jesus. Before his encounter with Christ, Paul was a man filled with hatred and violence, seeking to destroy the very people he would later call his brothers and sisters in Christ. But once he met Jesus, everything changed. His heart was filled with love and compassion, and his greatest desire was to help others experience the same transformation he had. This happens when we encounter Jesus: our lives are given new meaning and purpose. We are no longer living for ourselves but for the glory of God and the advancement of His Kingdom.

In a world often filled with distractions and competing priorities, Paul's life is a reminder of what truly matters. His unwavering focus on Christ and His Kingdom shows us that living purposefully is about keeping our eyes on Jesus and sharing His love with others. We, too, must make it our mission to proclaim that Jesus is God's Son, just as Paul did. Our lives have eternal significance when we live with this purpose. We are no longer just going through the motions of life; we are participating in the most incredible mission: bringing people into the Kingdom of God.

Paul's life was a testament to what can happen when someone is fully consumed to enlarge Christ's Kingdom. He didn't allow fear, doubt, or opposition to stop him. Instead, he pressed on, knowing that every soul he reached with the gospel was another life changed for eternity. His boldness and determination inspire us to live with the same kind of passion and purpose. Like Paul, we are called to be Kingdom builders, spreading the message of Jesus wherever we go, knowing that it is the most important work we will ever do.

In conclusion, Paul's bold proclamation of Christ is a powerful example of what it means to live with purpose. From the moment he met Jesus, Paul knew that his life was no longer about him; it was about sharing the truth of Christ with the world. He preached boldly, faced opposition with courage, and proved through Scripture that Jesus is the Son of God. His life was consumed with the mission of enlarging Christ's Kingdom, and he did so without hesitation or fear. We, too, are called to live with this purpose, focusing on the core message of the gospel and sharing it with the world. Like Paul, we must be willing to step out in faith, knowing that the message of Christ is worth any cost.

Chapter 2 – Powerful

Paul's journey as a Kingdom builder was marked by incredible growth in spiritual strength and boldness. After his radical encounter with Jesus on the road to Damascus, Paul (formerly known as Saul) became a powerful voice for Christ. Acts 9:22 tells us, "But Saul increased the more in strength, and confounded the Jews... proving that this is very Christ." This verse captures the essence of Paul's ministry — he grew stronger each day, not just in his physical endurance but in his spiritual conviction and ability to share the gospel in a way that left people astonished and unable to refute his message. From the start of his ministry, Paul's mission was to make Jesus known, and as he preached, he relied on the Holy Spirit to guide him, strengthen him, and give him the wisdom and power needed to face opposition and prove the truth of Christ's identity.

Paul's bold proclamation of Christ wasn't just about words; it was backed by a deep spiritual authority from his relationship with God. The more he relied on the Holy Spirit, the more his strength grew, and with that strength came the ability to defend the gospel in powerful ways. He confounded those who opposed him, not because of his intellect or skill, but because the truth of Christ was undeniable, and the Spirit of God was at work through him. Paul's growth in strength was a reflection of his deepening faith and trust in God. He knew that the message he was preaching was not something he had come up with on his own — it was the truth of who Jesus was, the Son of God, the Messiah who had come to save the world. As each day passed, Paul became more confident in that truth, giving him the courage to stand firm, no matter his challenges.

As Paul continued to grow in strength, he faced increasing opposition. The Jews who heard him were confounded — they couldn't believe that the same man who had once persecuted Christians was now their most powerful advocate. Paul's transformation was so complete and radical that it left people speechless. But Paul didn't let their confusion or hostility deter him. Instead, he pressed on, proving through Scripture and reason that Jesus was indeed the Christ. This wasn't an easy task, but Paul's growing strength in the Spirit allowed him to persevere. He wasn't preaching for personal gain or recognition; he was driven by a deep conviction that the gospel was the most crucial message anyone could hear. And because of that, he was willing to face whatever opposition came his way.

Paul's power in his ministry wasn't his own — it came from the Holy Spirit. This is a crucial lesson for all believers. Like Paul, we are called to rely on the power of the Holy Spirit to grow in strength and confidently defend the truth of the gospel. We can't do it on our own. Our strength, like Paul's, comes from God. When we trust in Him, He equips us with everything we need to stand firm in our faith and share the message of Christ with boldness. Paul's life is a powerful example of what can happen when we rely entirely on the Holy Spirit. He didn't rely on his abilities or past experiences; he leaned into the power of God, and because of that, he could accomplish incredible things for the Kingdom.

Paul's growth in strength also speaks to the importance of perseverance in the Christian life. He didn't become strong overnight — it was a process that required faith, endurance, and a willingness to keep going even when things got tough. Each time Paul faced opposition, he grew more assertive. Each time he was challenged, his faith deepened. This is a lesson for all of us. Growth in spiritual strength doesn't happen in a vacuum; it occurs in challenges, trials, and opposition. But when we rely on the Holy Spirit, those challenges become growth opportunities. Just as Paul's strength increased as he faced opposition, so too can our strength grow as we trust God in difficulties. The more we lean on Him, the stronger we become, and the more confident we can be in our ability to stand firm in our faith and share the truth of Christ with the world.

Paul's ability to prove that Jesus was Christ is also a powerful reminder of the importance of knowing the Scriptures and being able to defend our faith. Paul didn't just proclaim the gospel; he was able to prove it through Scripture and reason. He knew the Word of God and used it to show others the truth of who Jesus was. This is something that all believers should strive for. We need to know the Scriptures to defend our faith and prove the gospel's truth to those who may doubt or oppose it. But again, this is not something we can do on our own. We need the Holy Spirit to give us wisdom and understanding to effectively share the gospel and prove the truth of Christ to those who need to hear it.

Paul's life testified to the power of the Holy Spirit in a believer's life. He started his ministry with boldness, and as he grew in strength, that boldness only increased. He didn't shrink back in the face of opposition; he pressed on, knowing his message was worth any cost. His confidence wasn't in himself but in the God who had called and empowered him to share the gospel. And because of that confidence, Paul could prove the truth of Christ in a way that left his opponents speechless. This is the kind of confidence we should all aspire to. When we rely on the Holy Spirit, we can stand firm in our faith, knowing that God will give us the strength to share and defend the gospel against those who oppose it.

In Acts 9:22, we see the beginning of Paul's journey of growing strength. He wasn't content to stay where he was; he wanted to grow, to become stronger in his faith, and to be more effective in his ministry. This desire to grow is something that all believers should have. We should never be content with where we are in our faith; we should always seek to grow stronger, know God more deeply, and effectively share the gospel. But again, this growth is not something we can achieve on our own. It comes from relying on the Holy Spirit and allowing Him to work in our lives. Just as Paul grew in strength, we can grow as we trust God and seek to live out our faith with boldness and confidence.

Paul's life is a powerful example of what it means to rely on the power of the Holy Spirit. He didn't start his ministry with all the answers or the strength he would need to face the challenges ahead. But as he trusted in God and relied on the Holy Spirit, he grew stronger each day. His confidence in the gospel's truth allowed him to stand firm, even in intense opposition. And because of that confidence, Paul could prove the truth of Christ to those who doubted. This is a reminder to all of us that we don't have to have it all figured out. We must trust in God, rely on the Holy Spirit, and allow Him to work. As we do, we will grow more robust, and we will be able to share the gospel with the same boldness and confidence that Paul displayed.

In conclusion, Paul's life as a Kingdom builder was marked by his growing strength in the Spirit and his bold proclamation of Christ. He didn't rely on his abilities or strength; he trusted the Holy Spirit to guide, strengthen, and give him the wisdom and power to share and defend the gospel against opposition. As believers, we, too, are called to rely on the power of the Holy Spirit to grow in strength and to uphold the truth of the gospel with confidence. Paul's example teaches us that growth in spiritual strength comes through perseverance, reliance on God, and a deep commitment to sharing the truth of Christ. When we follow Paul's example and rely on the Holy Spirit, we can stand firm in our faith and boldly proclaim the gospel's truth to a world in need.

Chapter 3 – Persistent

Paul's life was a remarkable story of persistence, marked by his unwavering determination to share the gospel no matter what came his way. After his transformative encounter with Christ, Paul became a Kingdom builder, committed to proclaiming the truth of Jesus as the Son of God. Acts 9:22 says, "Saul increased the more in strength... proving that this is very Christ." This verse captures the essence of Paul's ministry — his relentless persistence in spreading the message of Christ. Paul didn't just start strong; he grew stronger and more determined with every step despite his many trials and opposition. His persistence was not driven by pride or personal ambition but by a deep conviction that the truth of Christ was worth any cost. Paul knew that the gospel was the only message that could save lives and bring people into a relationship with God, and that belief gave him the courage to keep going, even when the road ahead seemed impossible.

From the moment Paul began preaching, he faced resistance. His sudden transformation confounded the Jews in Damascus. How could the man who once persecuted Christians now be one of their most passionate advocates? People doubted him, questioned his motives, and even sought to kill him, but none of that could shake Paul's resolve. His persistence was rooted in the strength of God, not his abilities. With each challenge, Paul's faith grew more profound, and his spiritual strength increased. He wasn't content to let fear or opposition hold him back. Instead, he pressed on, proving through Scripture and reason that Jesus was indeed the Christ. Paul's ability to stand firm in the face of opposition was a testament to his character and the power of the Holy Spirit at work in him. He knew he wasn't fighting these battles alone; God was with him every step of the way, giving him the strength he needed to persist.

Paul's persistence wasn't just about continuing to preach when things got tough; it was about growing stronger through those difficulties. The more he was challenged, the more he increased in strength. This is a powerful lesson for all believers. When we face opposition, it's easy to want to give up or back down. But Paul's life shows us that we have the most significant opportunity to grow in those moments of challenge. Each time Paul encountered resistance, he became more confident in the truth of the gospel and more determined to share it with others. His persistence was fueled by his deep understanding of who Jesus was and the importance of his message. He knew that the gospel was too important to be silenced by opposition, and that gave him the courage to keep going, even when it seemed like the whole world was against him.

As believers, we can take great encouragement from Paul's example. Just like Paul, we are called to continue sharing the gospel, even when faced with challenges or opposition. It's easy to share our faith when things are going well, but what about when people mock or reject the message? What about facing opposition from those closest to us or when the world seems against us? It's in those moments that our persistence is tested. Paul's life shows us that we don't have to fear opposition. Instead, we can trust that God will strengthen us, just as He did for Paul. The same God who empowered Paul to persist in his ministry is the same God who is with us today, giving us the strength we need to keep going.

His unwavering focus on Christ also marked Paul's persistence. He didn't let the world's distractions distract him from his mission. His purpose was clear: proclaiming Jesus as the Christ, the Son of God, and bringing as many people as possible into the Kingdom. He didn't let the fear of rejection or persecution stop him from fulfilling that purpose. The more opposition he faced, the more determined he became. This reminds us that persistence is not just about continuing to do something; it's about doing it with a clear purpose and determination. Paul wasn't just going through the motions; he was fully committed to God's mission and willing to endure whatever it took to fulfill it.

As Paul's strength grew, so did his ability to prove that Jesus was the Christ. He didn't just preach the gospel; he backed it up with Scripture and reason, confounding those who opposed him. This shows us the importance of knowing the Word of God and being able to defend our faith. Paul's persistence wasn't just about continuing to preach; it was about growing in his ability to share the gospel effectively. He wasn't content just telling people about Jesus; he wanted to prove to them, through Scripture, that Jesus fulfilled the prophecies and was the world's Saviour. This is a powerful example for all of us. As we persist in sharing the gospel, we should also grow in our understanding of Scripture and our ability to share the truth of Christ in a way that makes sense to those who hear it.

Paul's persistence also teaches us the importance of trusting God in the face of opposition. Paul didn't rely on his strength or abilities; he relied on God. He knew that without God's help, he couldn't accomplish the mission he had been given. But he also knew that with God, all things were possible. This is a crucial lesson for all of us. When we face challenges, it's easy to feel like we're not strong enough to keep going. But Paul's life shows us we don't have to rely on our strength. God is with us and will strengthen us just as He strengthened Paul. When we trust in God, we can face any opposition confidently, knowing He will give us the strength to persist.

Paul's story is also a reminder that persistence is not just about enduring difficulties but growing through them. Each time Paul faced opposition, he grew stronger in his faith and more confident in the truth of the gospel. This is a powerful example for all of us. When we face challenges in our lives, we have a choice: let those challenges discourage us or let them strengthen us. Paul chose the latter, and because of that, his ministry was incredibly effective. His persistence in the face of opposition allowed him to reach countless people with the message of Christ, and his strength grew with each challenge he faced.

In conclusion, Paul's life as a Kingdom builder was marked by incredible persistence. He didn't let opposition, rejection, or persecution stop him from proclaiming the truth of Christ. Instead, he grew stronger with each challenge, relying on the power of the Holy Spirit to give him the strength he needed to keep going. Paul's life is a powerful example for all believers. We are called to continue sharing the gospel, even when faced with challenges or opposition. We must trust that God will strengthen us, just as He strengthened Paul. The same God who empowered Paul to persist in his ministry is the same God who is with us today, giving us the strength we need to fulfill the mission He has given us. As we continue sharing the gospel, we should also grow in our understanding of Scripture and our ability to share Christ's truth effectively. Like Paul, we can face any challenge confidently, knowing that God is with us and will give us the strength to keep going.

Chapter 4 – Proclaimer

Once a fierce persecutor of Christians, Paul became one of the boldest proclaimers of the gospel, and the power of Christ transformed his entire life. From the beginning of his conversion, Paul was not content with remaining silent. Acts 9:20 says, "He preached Christ... that He is the Son of God." This statement defines Paul's mission, identity, and unrelenting passion for the rest of his life. Paul had a clear message: Jesus is the Son of God, and He is the Savior of the world. From the moment Paul encountered Jesus on the road to Damascus, he knew his life had one singular purpose—to proclaim this truth to everyone he encountered, no matter the cost. And Paul didn't wait to get started. Immediately after his conversion, he went into the synagogues, where he once sought to arrest Christians, and boldly proclaimed the very name he had once tried to destroy. His life became a testimony of the radical change when someone meets Jesus.

Paul's role as a proclaimer was not something he took lightly. He knew that proclaiming Jesus as the Son of God was the most crucial message anyone could hear, and he was willing to face whatever opposition came his way to share that truth. His message was simple yet profound: Jesus is the Son of God, sent by the Father to redeem humanity and offer eternal life. Paul understood this life-changing truth and dedicated his life to ensuring everyone heard it. He went from city to city, preaching in synagogues, homes, and public squares, telling anyone who would listen that Jesus was the promised Messiah, the fulfillment of the Scriptures, and the only way to salvation. Paul didn't care about the consequences; he was so overwhelmed by the truth of who Jesus was that he could not keep quiet. His heart burned with the desire to see people come to know Jesus as their Savior, and he was willing to face any danger, rejection, or hardship to proclaim the good news of Jesus Christ.

Paul's boldness in proclaiming Jesus as the Son of God was not just about standing up and speaking; it was about declaring the very essence of who Jesus is.

Paul knew that proclaiming Jesus meant declaring His divinity, power, authority, and love for all humanity. Paul didn't shy away from the fact that Jesus was not just a good teacher or prophet but God in the flesh. This truth sets Paul's message apart and makes it so powerful. Paul was proclaiming the truth that God Himself had come to earth in the person of Jesus, lived a perfect life, died on the cross for our sins, and rose again to conquer death. This was the message that Paul was willing to give his life for, and it's the same message that can change lives today.

From the moment Paul began preaching, he faced intense opposition. People didn't want to hear that Jesus was the Son of God, especially those who had rejected Him during His earthly ministry. But Paul didn't back down. He knew that proclaiming the truth about Jesus would not always be popular, but it was always necessary. His unwavering commitment to proclaiming Christ, even in the face of danger, is a powerful example for all believers today. We, too, are called to proclaim the good news of Jesus, to declare His divinity and His saving power to a world that desperately needs to hear it. Like Paul, we must be willing to face opposition, rejection, and hardship if necessary, knowing that the message we carry is too important to remain silent.

Paul's proclamation of Jesus was not just about words but the power of the message. He didn't just preach; he lived out the gospel in every aspect of his life. His boldness, his perseverance, his love for others—all of these things reflected the truth of who Jesus is. Paul's life became a living proclamation of the gospel, and people couldn't deny the power of the message because they saw it lived out in him. This is a challenge for all of us. Proclaiming Jesus is not just about what we say; it's about how we live. Our lives should reflect the gospel, showing others the love, grace, and truth of Jesus in everything we do. When people see the power of Christ at work in our lives, it gives credibility to our message.

Paul's declaration that Jesus is the Son of God was also deeply rooted in Scripture. He didn't rely on his own experience to convince others of the truth; he used the Word of God to prove that Jesus was the fulfillment of the Scriptures and the promised Messiah. As believers, we are called to proclaim Jesus to the world, but we must also be able to back up our proclamation with the truth of Scripture. When we proclaim Jesus as the Son of God, we are not just sharing our opinions but declaring the unchanging truth of God's Word. Paul's example shows us the importance of faith in Scripture to share the gospel and lead others to the truth effectively.

Paul's life as a proclaimer of Christ was not just a momentary phase but a lifelong commitment. He didn't just proclaim Jesus when it was convenient, or people were receptive to the message. He proclaimed Jesus in every circumstance, whether free to preach in synagogues or locked up in prison. Paul's commitment to proclaiming Christ was unwavering and didn't depend on his circumstances. This is a powerful lesson for all of us. We are called to proclaim Jesus in every season of life, whether things are going well or facing difficulties. Our circumstances should never dictate our commitment to proclaiming the truth of who Jesus is. Like Paul, we must be willing to proclaim Jesus in every situation, trusting that God will use our faithfulness to reach others with the gospel.

Paul's proclamation of Christ was not just about reaching the Jews; he was determined to take the message of Jesus to the Gentiles as well. Paul understood that the good news of Jesus was for all people, and he was relentless in his pursuit of sharing that message with everyone, regardless of their background or culture. Paul's heart for the lost was evident in the way he traveled to distant lands, endured hardship, and faced persecution to ensure that people everywhere had the opportunity to hear the gospel. His life was a testament to the fact that proclaiming Jesus is not limited by borders, cultures, or languages. The message of Jesus is for everyone, and we, like Paul, are called to take that message to the ends of the earth. Whether we are called to share the gospel in our neighborhoods or faraway places, we must be willing to go wherever God leads us and proclaim Jesus to all who need to hear it.

Paul's unwavering commitment to proclaiming Jesus as the Son of God was not without cost. He faced beatings, imprisonment, rejection, and even the threat of death. But none of that stopped him. Paul understood that proclaiming the truth of Jesus was worth any price. He was willing to give up everything for the gospel's sake because he knew his message could change lives and bring people into a relationship with God. Paul's example challenges us to consider the cost of following Jesus and proclaiming His name. Are we willing to face opposition, endure hardship, or sacrifice our comfort to proclaim the good news of Jesus? Paul's life shows us that the cost is worth it because the message of Jesus is the most crucial message anyone could ever hear.

In conclusion, Paul's life as a proclaimer of Christ is a powerful example for all believers. From the moment of his conversion, Paul was consumed with the desire to proclaim Jesus as the Son of God, and he spent the rest of his life sharing that truth with everyone he encountered. His boldness, perseverance, and unwavering commitment to the gospel inspire all who follow Christ. Like Paul, we are called to proclaim Jesus' divinity and the message of salvation to a world that desperately needs to hear it. We must be willing to face opposition, endure hardship, and live out the truth of the gospel in every aspect of our lives. Paul's life reminds us that proclaiming Jesus is not just a task for a select few; it is the calling of every believer. We are all called to proclaim the good news, sharing the truth of who Jesus is and what He has done for us with the world. Like Paul, let us be bold in our proclamation, trusting that God will use our faithfulness to bring others into His Kingdom.

Chapter 5 – Prepared

Paul's life was a testimony to the power of being prepared by God for a great purpose. From the moment he encountered Jesus on the road to Damascus, Paul's entire life changed, and he became fully equipped to preach the gospel with boldness. Acts 9:27 tells us how Barnabas vouched for Paul, explaining to the apostles that Paul had seen the Lord and had already begun preaching boldly in Damascus. This verse is a powerful reminder that Paul was not hesitant or unsure about his mission—he was ready from the very beginning, prepared by Christ Himself to take on the role of a Kingdom builder. Paul's preparation didn't come from years of training or human wisdom but from a direct and personal calling from Jesus. That moment on the road to Damascus was Paul's preparation. Jesus revealed Himself to Paul, changed his heart, and gave him a clear purpose: to proclaim the good news to all, even to the ends of the earth. From that moment on, Paul was ready to step into his calling boldly.

Paul's preparation was unique because it came straight from Christ. He didn't wait to be approved by others or to gain more experience. Instead, he immediately began preaching about Jesus in Damascus, boldly declaring that Jesus was the Son of God. Paul knew that the calling on his life was not something he had chosen for himself—it was something God had chosen for him. And because of that, he didn't hesitate. He didn't need to rely on his past knowledge or accomplishments; instead, he relied entirely on the fact that Jesus had called him, which was all the preparation he needed. This is a compelling example for us today. We often feel unprepared or inadequate for the tasks God has called us to, but Paul's life shows us that when God calls us, He also equips us. We don't need to have everything figured out or feel completely ready; we just need to trust that God has prepared us for the work He has set before us.

From the moment Paul began preaching in Damascus, it was clear that God had equipped him for the task. He wasn't just speaking words but preaching boldly and powerfully. This boldness didn't come from Paul's natural abilities but from God's preparation. When Barnabas spoke to the apostles on Paul's behalf, he didn't just mention Paul's past or knowledge; he highlighted Paul's boldness in preaching the gospel. This boldness directly resulted from the preparation Paul had received from Christ. God had called Paul and filled him with the courage and confidence to step into that calling without hesitation. Paul wasn't concerned about his past as a persecutor of Christians or how people might receive his message. He knew that God had prepared him for this moment, and that was all that mattered.

Paul's preparation also involved a profound transformation of his heart. Before his encounter with Jesus, Paul had been zealous in his persecution of Christians. He had excellent knowledge and passion, but his zeal was misguided. After meeting Jesus, however, Paul's heart was changed entirely. The same zeal he once had for persecuting Christians was now directed toward preaching the gospel and building Christ's Kingdom. This transformation was part of Paul's preparation. God didn't just call him to a new mission; He changed his heart and gave him a new purpose. Paul's past no longer defined him; instead, his life was now defined by his calling to proclaim the good news of Jesus. This is a powerful reminder that when God prepares us for His work, He doesn't just equip us with the needed skills; He transforms our hearts to align with His purposes.

One of the most incredible aspects of Paul's preparation is that it was immediate. When Paul encountered Jesus, he didn't wait to start preaching. He didn't spend years studying or training before stepping into his calling. Instead, he began preaching in the synagogues, boldly declaring that Jesus was the Son of God. This shows us that when God prepares us for a task, we don't have to wait until we feel "ready" in the traditional sense. Paul's readiness came from his encounter with Christ, and that was enough. He trusted God had given him everything he needed to begin his ministry immediately. This is a lesson for all of us. When God calls us to something, we may not feel fully prepared in our strength, but we can trust that God has already given us what we need to step into that calling with boldness.

Paul's boldness in preaching directly resulted from his confidence in his calling. He knew his encounter with Jesus was real, assuring him to proclaim the gospel without fear. This confidence didn't come from Paul's abilities or knowledge but from knowing Christ had personally called and equipped him.

Paul's life is a powerful example of what it looks like to trust in God's preparation fully. He didn't doubt his calling or hesitate to enter it because God had already given him everything he needed. This boldness comes when we genuinely believe He has prepared us for the work He has called us to do. When we have that confidence, we can step into any situation, no matter how difficult or intimidating, and boldly proclaim the truth of who Jesus is.

Paul's preparation also involved the support of others. While Paul was personally called and equipped by Christ, he also had the support of people like Barnabas, who vouched for him and helped him gain acceptance among the apostles. This shows us that God often uses others to affirm and support our calling. Even though Paul Christ was fully prepared, Paul still needed the encouragement and support of other believers. Barnabas played a crucial role in helping Paul step into his ministry, and this reminds us that we are not meant to walk in our calling alone. God often places people in our lives who can help us, encourage us, and affirm the work He is doing in us. This is an essential part of the preparation process. While God is the one who ultimately equips us for His work, He often uses the people around us to help us grow and step into that calling with boldness.

Paul's life is a powerful example of what it looks like to be fully prepared by God for a specific purpose. His encounter with Jesus was the defining moment of his life, and from that moment on, he was ready to proclaim the gospel to everyone he encountered boldly. Paul didn't need years of preparation or training; he was prepared from the outset because God had personally called and equipped him. This is a powerful reminder that when God calls us to something, He prepares us for it. We don't have to rely on our abilities or feel we need to figure everything out. God's preparation is enough, and when we trust in that, we can step into our calling with boldness and confidence.

We can all learn from Paul's boldness in preaching the gospel. He didn't let fear or doubt hold him back. He trusted that God had prepared him for the task at hand, which gave him the courage to step into his calling confidently. This is a lesson for all of us. We often feel inadequate or unprepared for what God calls us to do, but Paul's life shows us that when God calls us, He also equips us. We don't need to wait until we feel ready or have all the answers; we just need to trust that God has already given us everything we need to step into that calling with boldness.

Paul's preparation also reminds us that God often uses our past experiences, even the difficult ones, to prepare us for the work He has called us to do. Paul's past as a persecutor of Christians could have disqualified him from ministry in the eyes of many, but God used Paul's past to shape him into the powerful proclaimer of the gospel that he became. God didn't waste any part of Paul's story. Instead, He redeemed it and used it for His glory. This is a powerful reminder that no matter what our past looks like, God can use it as part of His preparation for the work He has called us to do. Our past doesn't define us; our calling from God does.

In conclusion, Paul's life is a powerful example of what it looks like to be fully prepared by God for a specific purpose. From the moment he encountered Jesus, Paul was ready to proclaim the gospel to everyone he encountered boldly. His preparation didn't come from years of training or human wisdom but from Christ's direct and personal calling. Paul's boldness, confidence, and unwavering commitment to his calling are a powerful reminder that when God calls us, He also equips us. We don't need to rely on our abilities or feel we need to figure everything out. God's preparation is enough; when we trust that, we can step into our calling with boldness and confidence, just like Paul.

Chapter 6 – Passionate

Paul's passion for Christ was undeniable. Paul's life was radically transformed from encountering Jesus on the road to Damascus. He went from being a fierce persecutor of Christians to one of the most passionate and bold proclaimers of the gospel the world has ever known. Acts 9:27 tells us that Paul "preached boldly at Damascus in the name of Jesus," and this verse captures the fire that burned within him. Paul was not hesitant, nor did he hold back in his preaching. His passion for Christ fueled his every word and action. He had experienced the grace of God firsthand, and that experience lit a fire in his heart that could not be extinguished. Paul was a man who was wholly consumed by the love of Christ and the truth of the gospel, and that passion was evident in everything he did. He was unashamed and unafraid to speak the truth about Jesus, no matter the cost. His boldness in proclaiming Christ reflected his courage and deep love for the Savior who rescued him.

Paul's passion for Christ drove him to preach boldly, even in fierce opposition. In Damascus, where he had once sought to arrest Christians, he now stood boldly proclaiming the very name he had once sought to destroy. This transformation was not just a change of mind but a heart. Paul's passion for Jesus was born out of his deep gratitude for the grace and mercy he had received. He knew that he had been forgiven much and that forgiveness fueled his desire to share the message of salvation with everyone he encountered. Paul didn't hold back in his preaching because he knew his message was too important to be kept quiet. He was passionate about making sure that as many people as possible heard the good news of Jesus, and that passion gave him the boldness to preach without fear.

Paul's passion for Christ was so powerful that it was not driven by emotion alone; it was rooted in truth. Paul's passion was not a fleeting feeling that came and went with the circumstances. It was a deep, abiding commitment to the reality of who Jesus is and what He had done for Paul and the world. His understanding of the gospel fueled Paul's passion, which gave him the confidence to speak boldly. He knew that the message he was proclaiming was the truth, and that truth gave him the courage to stand firm, even when faced with opposition. Paul's passion for Christ was not about drawing attention to himself but pointing people to Jesus. He didn't preach to make a name for himself; he preached to make the name of Jesus known. This is a powerful lesson for all of us. Our passion for Christ should not be about us but about making Jesus known to a world that desperately needs to hear the truth.

Paul's passion was contagious. His boldness in proclaiming the gospel inspired others to follow his example and share the good news of Jesus with the same kind of passion and commitment. Paul's life shows us that passion is not just about how we feel; it's about how we live. Paul's passion for Christ was evident in how he lived his life. He was fully committed to sharing the gospel, and that commitment was unwavering. He didn't let fear or opposition stop him from proclaiming the truth; that passion inspired others to do the same. Paul's life reminds us that when we are passionate about something, it will be evident in how we live. Our passion for Christ should be apparent not just in our words but in our actions. We should live so that people can see the love of Jesus in everything we do.

Paul's passion for Christ was also marked by his willingness to suffer for the gospel's sake. He didn't just preach boldly when it was convenient or when people were receptive to his message. He preached boldly even when it cost him dearly. Paul faced persecution, imprisonment, and even death for the gospel's sake, but none of that could extinguish the fire within him. His passion for Christ was more substantial than his fear of suffering. He knew his message was worth any price, and that passion gave him the strength to endure whatever came his way. Paul's willingness to suffer for the gospel's sake is a powerful reminder that true love for Christ is not about seeking comfort or avoiding hardship. It's about laying down our lives to make Jesus known.

Paul's boldness in gospel preaching also reflected his deep love for people. He wasn't just passionate about Jesus but about seeing people come to know Jesus. Paul's heart broke for those who didn't know Christ, and that love for others fueled his desire to share the gospel with as many people as possible. Paul wasn't content with keeping the good news of Jesus to himself. He knew that people's eternal destinies were at stake, and that knowledge drove him to preach urgently and boldly. Paul's passion for Christ and his love for people were inseparable. He knew the most loving thing he could do for others was share the message of salvation with them, even if it meant facing rejection or persecution. Paul's life reminds us that our passion for Christ should be coupled with a deep love for others. We should be driven by a desire to see people come to know Jesus, and that desire should give us the courage to share the gospel boldly, no matter the cost.

Paul's passion for Christ was not something he kept to himself but passed on to others. He mentored and discipled others, encouraging them to share the gospel with the same kind of passion and boldness that he had. Paul's passion for Christ was not just about what he could accomplish but about raising others to continue sharing the gospel. Paul knew that the mission of spreading the good news of Jesus was more significant than him, and he was committed to equipping others to carry on that mission after he was gone. Paul's life reminds us that true passion for Christ is not just about what we can do; it's about investing in others and equipping them to carry on the work of the gospel.

His unwavering focus on the mission also marked Paul's passion for Christ. He didn't let distractions pull him away from his calling. He knew his purpose was to preach the gospel and was fully committed. Paul's passion for Christ gave him the clarity and focus he needed to stay on mission, even when the world around him was filled with distractions and temptations. This is a powerful lesson for all of us. In a world constantly pulling us in different directions, losing sight of what matters is easy. But Paul's life shows us that when we are passionate about Christ, we can stay focused on the mission, no matter what distractions come our way.

Paul's passion for Christ also gave him the resilience to keep going, even when things got tough. He didn't give up when he faced opposition or hardship. Instead, he pressed on, knowing his message was worth any cost. Paul's passion for Christ gave him the strength to endure, even in the face of overwhelming challenges. His life reminds us that passion is not just about how we start; it's about how we finish. Paul didn't just start strong; he finished strong. He remained passionate about Christ until the very end of his life, and that passion carried him through every trial and challenge he faced. Paul's life is a powerful reminder that true passion for Christ is not fleeting but a lifelong commitment.

In conclusion, Paul's life was a powerful example of what it means to be passionate about Christ. His boldness in preaching the gospel, willingness to suffer for Christ's sake, and unwavering commitment to making Jesus known stemmed from his deep passion for the Savior who rescued him. Paul's passion for Christ was about his words and how he lived his life. He was unashamed and unafraid to speak the truth about Jesus; that passion was evident in everything he did. Paul's life challenges us to examine our hearts. Are we passionate about Christ? Are we unashamed and unafraid to share the gospel with others? Are we willing to suffer for the sake of making Jesus known? Paul's life reminds us that true passion for Christ is not just about how we feel; it's about how we live. When we are genuinely passionate about Christ, that passion will be evident in every aspect of our lives, and it will give us the boldness and courage we need to share the good news of Jesus with a world that desperately needs to hear it. Like Paul, let us be passionate proclaimers of the gospel, unashamed and unafraid to speak the truth about Jesus, no matter the cost.

Chapter 7 – Proving

Paul's life was a testament to boldness and passion and his incredible ability to prove that Jesus was the Christ. Acts 9:22 tells us that Paul "proved that this is very Christ," meaning that Paul wasn't simply proclaiming the message of the gospel; he was backing it up with solid evidence. He was determined to speak about Jesus and demonstrate, through Scripture and sound reasoning, that Jesus was indeed the Messiah—the promised Savior of the world. Paul's ability to prove that Jesus was the Christ came from his deep knowledge of the Scriptures and his encounter with the risen Jesus. He didn't rely on blind faith alone; he knew that the truth of Jesus could be found throughout the Old Testament, and he was skilled in showing others how the life, death, and resurrection of Jesus fulfilled those prophecies. Paul's approach to proving the gospel wasn't based on emotional appeals or abstract ideas but on facts, Scripture, and logical reasoning, leaving his audience without room for doubt.

From his conversion, Paul had a burning desire to preach the gospel and help people see clearly that Jesus fulfilled God's promise. His heart was set on showing both Jews and Gentiles that Jesus was the long-awaited Messiah, and he was relentless in proving it to anyone who would listen. In the synagogues of Damascus, Paul began his ministry by confounding those who heard him. He didn't just speak about his personal experience with Jesus; he opened up the Scriptures and demonstrated how everything pointed to Jesus. His arguments were so compelling that even those who opposed him had difficulty refuting his claims. Paul's knowledge of Scripture and his passionate commitment to Christ made him a powerful advocate for the gospel.

Paul's life teaches us the importance of proving what we believe. It's not enough to simply declare that Jesus is Lord; we need to be able to explain why we believe that Jesus is the Messiah, using Scripture and reason to help others understand the truth. Paul's method was simple: he used the very Scriptures that his audience knew and respected to show that Jesus was the fulfillment of the promises made to Israel. He walked them through the prophecies, showing how Jesus's birth, life, death, and resurrection matched the expectations of the Messiah. Paul wasn't satisfied with vague assertions; he provided concrete evidence that could not be easily dismissed. This approach not only strengthened the faith of believers but also challenged nonbelievers to reconsider their views. Paul's ability to prove that Jesus was the Christ was not just for intellectuals but for everyone. His method of using Scripture and reason made the gospel accessible and understandable to everyone, regardless of their background.

One of the most remarkable aspects of Paul's ministry was his ability to adapt his message depending on his audience. When speaking to Jews, he used the Old Testament Scriptures to prove that Jesus was the Messiah. When talking to Gentiles, he used logical reasoning and even referenced cultural touchpoints to make his case. Paul understood that proving the truth of the gospel required a deep understanding of Scripture and an awareness of who he was speaking to. His ability to meet people where they were and present the gospel in a way that they could understand and relate to was one of the reasons his ministry was so effective. Paul knew it wasn't enough just to proclaim the gospel; he had to prove its truth in a way that made sense to the people he spoke to. This is a powerful lesson for all of us. When we share the gospel, we should be prepared to explain why we believe what we believe, using Scripture and reason to make a compelling case for Christ.

Paul's commitment to proving the truth of the gospel was not just about winning arguments but also leading people to a saving knowledge of Jesus. He wasn't interested in debating for the sake of arguing. His goal was always to bring people into a relationship with Christ. Paul's deep love for others drove him to spend countless hours reasoning with people, answering their questions, and showing them through Scripture and logic that Jesus responded to their deepest needs. He didn't shy away from difficult conversations or complex theological issues. Instead, he leaned into those challenges, confident that the truth of the gospel could stand up to any scrutiny. Paul knew that the stakes were high. He understood that people's eternal destinies were on the line and that knowledge gave him the perseverance to prove that Jesus was the Christ, even in the face of intense opposition.

Paul's ability to prove the gospel didn't just come from his knowledge of Scripture; it came from his personal experience with Jesus. Paul's encounter with the risen Christ on the road to Damascus was the foundation of his faith, and that experience gave him the confidence to prove to others that Jesus was alive. He knew that Jesus was the Christ because the Scriptures said so and because he had personally met Him. This combination of personal experience and deep scriptural knowledge made Paul a compelling witness for Christ. He didn't just speak from a place of intellectual knowledge but from a place of deep personal conviction. This reminds us that proving the truth of the gospel isn't just about knowing the right verses or having the correct arguments; it's about having a real, living relationship with Jesus that gives us the confidence to share Him with others.

Paul's approach to proving that Jesus was Christ also reminds us of the importance of being patient and persistent in sharing the gospel. Paul didn't expect people to accept everything he said immediately. He knew that proving the truth of the gospel sometimes required time, careful reasoning, and ongoing conversations. Paul was willing to spend as much time as necessary to help people understand the truth. He didn't give up on people when they didn't immediately believe. Instead, he kept proving, explaining, and demonstrating through Scripture and reason that Jesus was the Messiah. Paul's persistence in establishing the gospel is a challenge to all of us. We live in a world that is often skeptical of Christianity, and we need to be prepared to patiently and lovingly show people the truth, even when it takes time.

Paul's life also shows us that proving the truth of the gospel doesn't mean we have to have all the answers. Paul wasn't afraid to admit when he didn't know something, but he always pointed people back to the Scriptures and the person of Jesus. He understood that the gospel wasn't about having perfect knowledge but knowing the One who is the Truth. Paul's confidence in proving the gospel didn't come from his intellect or abilities but from his faith in Jesus and reliance on the Holy Spirit. This is an essential lesson for all of us. We don't have to have all the answers to prove that Jesus is the Christ. We just need to be faithful in sharing the truth of the gospel and trust that God will use our efforts to open people's hearts and minds to the truth.

In conclusion, Paul's life is a powerful example of what it means to prove that Jesus is the Christ. He didn't just proclaim the gospel; he backed it up with Scripture and reason, showing people clearly and convincingly that Jesus fulfilled God's promises. Paul's deep knowledge of the Scriptures and his personal experience with Jesus made him a powerful witness to the gospel. He could meet people where they were and present the gospel's truth in a way they could understand. Paul's life reminds us that we, too, are called to be prepared to give a reason for our hope, using Scripture and reason to help others understand the truth. Proving the gospel is not about winning arguments or being the most intelligent person in the room; it's about helping people see the beauty and truth of who Jesus is. Like Paul, let us be passionate about proving the gospel, patient in our efforts to share the truth, and confident that the message of Christ can stand up to any scrutiny. When we follow Paul's example, we can be convinced that God will use our efforts to bring others to a saving knowledge of Jesus.

Chapter 8 – Persevering

Paul's life was the perfect example of perseverance. From the moment he encountered Christ on the road to Damascus, his path was not easy, but he was determined to fulfill his calling. Acts 9:29 tells us that Paul "spake boldly in the name of the Lord Jesus, and disputed against the Grecians: but they went about to slay him." This verse captures the essence of Paul's relentless commitment to preaching Christ, even when his life was in danger. Paul faced constant threats, opposition, and persecution, but none of that could stop him from boldly proclaiming the name of Jesus. He didn't back down, he didn't shy away, and he didn't lose heart. No matter how fierce the persecution or high stakes were, Paul pressed on, fueled by an unshakable faith and a deep love for Christ. His perseverance in the face of danger is a powerful reminder of what it truly means to be a follower of Jesus, willing to endure hardship for the sake of the gospel.

From the very beginning of his ministry, Paul knew that following Christ would not be easy. He had once been the one persecuting Christians, and now he found himself on the other side, facing the very dangers he had once inflicted on others. But Paul didn't let fear dictate his actions. He knew that the message of Jesus was too important to keep silent, and he was willing to risk everything to make sure that people heard the truth. The Grecians, who opposed his message, sought to kill him, but Paul continued to preach boldly. Their threats didn't intimidate him because he knew his life was in God's hands. His perseverance came from a deep trust in God's sovereignty, knowing that the gospel would advance no matter what happened to him.

Paul's perseverance wasn't just about enduring physical danger and staying faithful to his mission despite hardships. He survived imprisonment, beatings, shipwrecks, and constant rejection, yet he never gave up. His heart was set on sharing the good news of Jesus with as many people as possible, and he was willing to go to any length to fulfill that calling. Paul's perseverance was driven by his love for Christ and his desire to see others come to know Him. He wasn't motivated by a need for personal recognition or success but by a deep sense of purpose. He knew that the gospel was worth any cost and that knowledge gave him the strength to keep going, no matter how difficult the road became.

One of Paul's most remarkable aspects of perseverance was his ability to keep preaching boldly, even when his life was constantly at risk. When faced with threats to their lives, most people would understandably be tempted to back down or find a safer path. But not Paul. He understood that the message of Christ was worth more than his safety. He didn't let the fear of death silence him. Instead, he continued to speak the truth, knowing that his time on earth was in God's hands. Paul's perseverance wasn't just about surviving persecution but thriving in his mission despite it. He didn't just endure hardship; he used it as an opportunity to glorify God and advance the gospel. His life is a powerful testimony that God's strength is made perfect in our weakness. Paul knew that he couldn't persevere on his own, but he also knew that with God's help, he could endure anything.

Paul's perseverance also speaks to the power of hope. He endured so much because he had an unshakable hope in the promises of God. He knew his future was secure in Christ no matter what he faced. That hope gave him the strength to keep going, even when the circumstances seemed overwhelming. Paul's eyes were fixed on eternity, and that eternal perspective helped him persevere through the temporary trials of this world. He wasn't focused on the here and now but on the glory that awaited him in heaven. This is a powerful lesson for all believers. When we fix our eyes on eternity and trust in the promises of God, we can persevere through even the most difficult challenges. Paul's hope in Christ was his anchor, and that hope sustained him through every trial he faced.

Paul's life also shows us that perseverance is not something we achieve on our own; it's something that God works in us. Paul's ability to endure persecution and hardship didn't come from his strength or determination but from the power of the Holy Spirit working in him. Paul was utterly dependent on God for the strength to persevere. He knew that he couldn't endure the trials of this life on his own, but he also knew that God's grace was sufficient for him. This is a powerful reminder for all of us. When we face hardship, persecution, or trials, we don't have to rely on our strength to get through it. God is with us and will give us the strength to persevere. Just as He did for Paul, He will sustain us through whatever we face.

Paul's perseverance reminds us that following Christ is not a path of comfort and ease. Jesus Himself said that following Him would mean taking up our cross daily, and Paul's life is a living example of what that looks like. Paul didn't expect an easy road; he knew that following Jesus meant suffering for the sake of the gospel. But he also knew that the suffering he experienced in this life was nothing compared to the glory that awaited him in eternity. Paul's perseverance challenges us to examine our own lives and ask ourselves whether we are willing to endure hardship for the sake of Christ. Are we willing to persevere in our faith, even when facing persecution or difficulty? Paul's life shows us that it's worth it. The gospel is worth any cost, and the reward of knowing Christ is far greater than any suffering we might endure in this life.

Paul's perseverance also reminds us that we are not alone in our struggles. Throughout his ministry, Paul had the support of other believers who encouraged him, prayed for him, and stood by him in his trials. Paul wasn't a lone wolf; he was part of a community of believers who shared his mission and supported him. This is an essential lesson for all of us. When we face hardship, we need the support and encouragement of other believers to help us persevere. We are called to bear one another's burdens and to encourage each other in our faith. Paul's life shows us the importance of community in our perseverance. We are stronger when we stand together, and God often encourages others to help us keep going when we feel like giving up.

In conclusion, Paul's life is a powerful example of what it means to persevere in the face of persecution and hardship. His boldness in preaching the gospel, even when his life was at risk, shows us what it looks like to be fully committed to Christ, no matter the cost. Paul's perseverance wasn't just about enduring physical danger and staying faithful to his mission, no matter his obstacles. His hope in Christ, reliance on God's strength, and willingness to suffer for the gospel's sake all fueled his perseverance. Paul's life challenges us to examine our commitment to Christ. Are we willing to persevere in our faith, even when facing persecution or hardship? Are we willing to keep proclaiming the name of Jesus, even when the world opposes us? Paul's life reminds us that the gospel is worth any cost and that with God's help, we can endure whatever comes our way. We are called to persevere, just as Paul did, trusting that God will give us the strength to stand firm in our faith and continue proclaiming the good news of Jesus to a world that desperately needs to hear it. Let us follow Paul's example and persevere in our faith, knowing that our hope in Christ is secure and that the reward of knowing Him is worth far more than anything we could ever lose in this life.

Chapter 9 - Persistent Boldness

Paul's life was a shining example of persistent boldness in proclaiming the name of Jesus. This boldness was unwavering and unshaken by the opposition, danger, or adversity he faced throughout his ministry. Acts 9:29 tells us, "He spake boldly in the name of the Lord Jesus," this one phrase captures the very heart of who Paul was and what drove him. Paul's life was transformed from encountering Jesus on the road to Damascus. He went from persecuting Christians to becoming one of the most courageous and outspoken voices for Christ. Paul didn't tiptoe around the truth. He didn't hold back out of fear of what others might think and wasn't afraid of the consequences of speaking the name of Jesus. His boldness wasn't a momentary flare of courage but a constant and consistent declaration of Christ's lordship in every situation he encountered. Whether preaching in the synagogues, debating with philosophers, or standing before kings, Paul's message was always the same: Jesus is Lord, and salvation is found in Him alone.

Paul's persistent boldness was rooted in his deep conviction that the gospel was the only truth that could set people free. He knew firsthand the transforming power of Jesus because his life had been radically changed. Before his conversion, Paul, then known as Saul, was zealous in his persecution of Christians. He thought he was doing the right thing by stamping out what he saw as a dangerous movement. But everything changed when Jesus appeared to him in a blinding light on the road to Damascus. Paul came face to face with the risen Christ, and in that moment, he realized that everything he had been fighting against was the truth. Jesus was the Messiah, the Son of God, and Paul had been persecuting the very one who came to save him. This life-changing encounter ignited a fire in Paul's heart that could never be extinguished. From that day forward, Paul lived with a singular mission: to proclaim the name of Jesus boldly, no matter the cost. Paul's boldness wasn't just about being brave but about being faithful. He understood that the message of the gospel was too important to keep to himself. He couldn't stay silent, even when it would have been safer or easier. Paul knew that people's eternal destinies were at stake and that knowledge drove him to speak boldly at every opportunity. He relentlessly spread the gospel because he knew Jesus was the only hope for a lost and broken world. His boldness wasn't fueled by pride or a desire for attention—it was driven by love. Paul loved Jesus with all his heart and loved people enough to risk everything to tell them about the Savior. This boldness can only come from a heart fully surrendered to Christ and willing to lay everything down for the gospel's sake.

Throughout his ministry, Paul faced intense opposition. He was beaten, imprisoned, mocked, and even stoned, yet he never backed down. His boldness was persistent because he knew his message was worth any sacrifice. No matter how many times he was thrown in prison, no matter how many times he was threatened with death, Paul continued to preach the name of Jesus. He was undeterred by the danger because he trusted in God's protection and guidance. Paul knew that as long as he was doing God's work, nothing could happen to him outside of God's will. This deep trust in God's sovereignty gave Paul the courage to speak boldly, even when the world was against him. He understood that his life was in God's hands and that knowledge gave him peace in every trial. Paul's unwavering trust in God is a powerful reminder to all of us that we, too, can speak boldly about Jesus, knowing that God is with us and will protect and guide us, no matter the circumstances.

Paul's persistent boldness also came from his unshakable belief in the power of the gospel. He knew that the message of Jesus had the power to transform lives because it had transformed his own life. He had experienced God's grace, forgiveness, and love so profoundly that he couldn't help but share it with others. Paul's boldness wasn't just about standing up to opposition; it was about offering hope to the hopeless, light to those in darkness, and life to the spiritually dead. He knew the gospel was the most powerful message the world had ever known, and he was determined to ensure that as many people as possible heard it. Paul didn't care whether people liked or hated him, whether they accepted or rejected his message—his job was to preach the truth, and he trusted God to do the rest. We are all called to have this kind of boldness as followers of Christ. We are not responsible for how people respond to the gospel but for sharing it boldly and without fear.

Paul's life is a powerful example of what it means to be bold for Christ, regardless of the circumstances. He didn't let fear of rejection or persecution stop him from proclaiming the name of Jesus. He didn't wait for the perfect moment or for a time when sharing the gospel would be easy or convenient. Paul spoke boldly at every opportunity because he knew the gospel was too important to wait. He understood that time was short and people needed to hear the truth now, not later. This sense of urgency drove Paul to preach the name of Jesus with boldness and persistence, no matter what obstacles he faced. His life challenges us to examine our boldness in sharing the gospel. Are we willing to speak boldly about Jesus, even when it's uncomfortable or risky? Are we willing to proclaim His name, even when it might cost us something?

Paul's boldness also reminds us that we don't have to be perfect or have all the answers to share the gospel. Paul didn't have it all figured out, but he knew one thing for sure: Jesus was the Son of God, and He had saved him. That was enough. Paul's boldness wasn't about his ability or knowledge but his faith in Jesus. He trusted that God would give him the words to say and the strength to face whatever came his way. This is a powerful reminder that we don't have to be experts to share the gospel. We just have to be willing. When we step out in faith and speak boldly about Jesus, God will equip us with everything we need. He will give us the words, the wisdom, and the courage to proclaim His name, just as He did for Paul.

Paul's persistent boldness wasn't just for his own time; it's a lesson for all of us today. We live in a world that is increasingly hostile to the message of Jesus, but that doesn't mean we should stay silent. If anything, it means we should be even more bold in proclaiming the truth. Just like Paul, we are called to speak boldly in the name of Jesus, trusting that God will protect us and guide us, no matter what opposition we face. The world needs to hear the gospel now more than ever, and it's up to us to share it boldly, just as Paul did. We may not face the same kind of physical persecution that Paul faced, but we will face opposition in many forms. But no matter what comes our way, we can trust that God is with us, just as He was with Paul.

In conclusion, Paul's life is a powerful example of persistent boldness in proclaiming the name of Jesus. Despite the dangers and opposition he faced, his unwavering commitment to preaching the gospel is a challenge and inspiration to all believers. Paul's boldness wasn't about his strength or ability but his deep trust in God and unshakable conviction that the gospel was the truth. He knew that the message of Jesus was too important to keep to himself, and he was willing to risk everything to make sure that people heard it. Paul's life reminds us that we, too, are called to speak boldly about Jesus, regardless of the circumstances. We don't have to be perfect or have all the answers; we just have to be willing to step out in faith and proclaim the name of Jesus with boldness. When we do, we can trust that God will protect us, guide us, and use us to bring His message of hope and salvation to a world that desperately needs to hear it. Like Paul, let us be persistent in our boldness, speak the name of Jesus without fear, and trust that God will be with us every step.

Chapter 10 – Partnership

Paul's life and ministry were defined by boldness, perseverance, and a deep, unwavering commitment to preaching the gospel of Jesus Christ. However, one of Paul's ministry's most critical and often overlooked aspects was his reliance on partnership. Even though Paul was known for his strength and independence, he didn't do his work alone. Acts 9:27 says, "Barnabas took him and brought him to the apostles," this verse reveals a critical truth: Paul's ministry involved others and thrived because of those partnerships. From the beginning of his Christian walk, Paul needed support, encouragement, and validation from fellow believers like Barnabas. Through partnerships like these, Paul grew in his ministry and fulfilled the calling that God had placed on his life. Paul's mission to spread the gospel was not a solo endeavor but a team effort, with many people coming alongside him to help build the Kingdom of God.

When Paul first became a Christian, he was met with skepticism and fear. The believers in Jerusalem were hesitant to accept him because of his past as a persecutor of Christians. They weren't sure if his conversion was genuine or if he could be trusted. However, Barnabas stepped in, stood by Paul's side, and vouched for him. Barnabas took Paul under his wing, introducing him to the apostles and helping to establish Paul's credibility among the believers. Without Barnabas' partnership, Paul may have struggled to find acceptance within the early Christian community. This moment of collaboration is significant because it reminds us that even the strongest and boldest leaders need the support and affirmation of others. Paul's ministry was launched partly because of Barnabas's willingness to take a risk, believe in him, and partner with him in spreading the gospel.

Partnership in ministry was not just something Paul experienced at the beginning of his journey; it was something that defined his entire ministry. Throughout his travels, Paul worked closely with other believers to establish churches, train leaders, and spread the message of Jesus. He partnered with Silas, Timothy, Priscilla, Aquila, and many others. Paul understood that the mission of spreading the gospel was too big for one person to handle alone. He recognized the value of working with others who shared the same vision and passion for the Kingdom of God. Paul was never too proud to ask for help or to rely on others. He knew that the church's strength lay in the unity and cooperation of its members, all working together for the common goal of advancing the gospel.

Paul's partnership with others also reveals the humility that marked his ministry. Even though he was a bold and confident preacher, Paul was always willing to acknowledge the contributions of others and to share the credit for the work being done. His letters frequently mentioned his fellow laborers, thanking them for their help and praising their faithfulness. Paul never saw himself as a lone hero or a one-person show. He knew his ministry's success was primarily due to the people who supported him, prayed for him, and worked alongside him. This is a powerful reminder that no matter how gifted or strong we may be, we all need the help of others to fulfill the calling God has placed on our lives. We were never meant to do ministry alone; we were created to work in partnership with other believers.

One of the most beautiful aspects of Paul's partnerships was the diversity of the people he worked with. Paul partnered with men and women, Jews and Gentiles, wealthy individuals, and humble servants. The gospel was for everyone, and Paul's ministry reflected that inclusivity. He didn't limit his partnerships to people like him but welcomed anyone willing to work for the Kingdom. This diversity in partnership demonstrates the heart of the gospel itself—that Jesus came to save people from every background, every culture, and every walk of life. Paul's willingness to work with such a diverse group shows us that the mission of spreading the gospel is not limited to one type of person or one way of doing things. Its mission requires all of us, with our unique gifts, talents, and perspectives, to work together to build the Kingdom of God.

Partnership in ministry also gave Paul the encouragement and accountability he needed to persevere through his many trials and hardships. Paul endured beatings, imprisonment, shipwrecks, and countless other challenges as he traveled from city to city preaching the gospel. In these difficult circumstances, the support of his fellow believers was a source of strength for him. Paul often mentioned how the prayers of the churches and the companionship of his fellow workers gave him the courage to keep going, even when the road was hard. This reminds us that we, too, need the encouragement of others to stay strong in our faith and to persevere in the work that God has called us to do. Ministry is not always easy, and we are bound to face challenges and opposition. But when we partner with other believers, we find the strength and encouragement to keep pressing on.

Paul's partnerships were not just about accomplishing a task but building relationships grounded in love and mutual respect. Paul wasn't just focused on the work; he cared deeply about the people he worked with. He invested in them, mentored them, and prayed for them. His letters are filled with love and gratitude for those who labored alongside him. Paul's partnerships were not transactional; they were relational. He understood that ministry was not just about getting the job done; it was about building up the body of Christ and strengthening one another in the faith. This is an essential lesson for all of us. When we partner with others in ministry, we are not just working toward a goal but building relationships that will last for eternity.

The partnership between Paul and Barnabas is also a reminder that ministry partnerships are not always easy. Later in their journey, Paul and Barnabas disagreed, leading them to separate. But even though their partnership ended, both men continued to serve God faithfully, and their disagreement didn't stop the work of the gospel. This teaches us that even in conflict, God can still use us to accomplish His purposes. We won't always agree with everyone we work with; sometimes, partnerships may end. But that doesn't mean that God's work stops. Paul and Barnabas continued to build the Kingdom, and God used their ministries to reach even more people with the gospel. This reminds us that God's plans are more significant than our disagreements, and even when partnerships don't last, the mission of spreading the gospel continues.

Paul's reliance on partnership also points us to the reality that we are part of a larger body—the body of Christ. None of us is called to do ministry in isolation. We are all members of the same body, and each has a unique role in building the Kingdom of God. Paul understood this deeply. He knew that he couldn't fulfill his calling alone, and he was willing to partner with others to accomplish the work that God had given him. This is a powerful reminder that we need each other. We need other believers' gifts, talents, and perspectives to accomplish the mission that God has given us entirely. No matter how strong or capable we may be, we are stronger together. Building the Kingdom of God is a collective effort; we can do far more than ever when we partner.

In conclusion, Paul's life and ministry are a powerful example of the importance of partnership in the work of the gospel. From the beginning of his journey as a follower of Christ, Paul relied on the support and encouragement of others like Barnabas to help him fulfill his calling. Throughout his ministry, Paul worked closely with other believers, recognizing that the mission of spreading the gospel was too big for one person to handle alone. His partnerships were grounded in love, mutual respect, and a shared commitment to the Kingdom of God. Paul's life challenges us to embrace partnership in our ministries, recognizing that we are part of a larger body working together to build the Kingdom. No matter how gifted or strong we may be, we need the support and encouragement of other believers to fulfill the calling that God has placed on our lives. Let us follow Paul's example and partner with one another in the work of the gospel, trusting that we can accomplish far more for the Kingdom than we ever could.

Chapter 11 – Pioneering

Paul's life was the ultimate example of pioneering for the sake of the gospel. From the beginning of his ministry until the end, Paul was constantly breaking new ground, forging new paths, and reaching people who had never heard the good news of Jesus Christ. Acts 28:31 says that Paul spent his final days "preaching the kingdom of God, and teaching those things which concern the Lord Jesus Christ." Even in the last chapter of his life, Paul was still boldly proclaiming the message of salvation, continuing his mission to spread the gospel to every corner of the world. His pioneering spirit was relentless, and his heart was fully committed to advancing the Kingdom of God, no matter the cost. Paul's entire ministry was defined by his willingness to go where no one else had gone, to reach those who had never heard, and to plant churches in places where the name of Jesus had not yet been spoken. He was a true trailblazer, laying the foundation for the early church's growth and setting the stage for the global spread of Christianity that continues today.

Paul's pioneering spirit began when he encountered Jesus on the road to Damascus. That encounter changed everything for him. Once a fierce persecutor of Christians, Paul became one of the gospel's most passionate and fearless proclaimers. However, Paul didn't limit his preaching to people already familiar with the Jewish faith or the message of Jesus. He was determined to take the gospel to new places, to people who had never heard the good news. Paul's pioneering spirit took him on countless journeys across the Roman Empire, where he preached to Jews and Gentiles alike, establishing churches and training leaders in cities like Ephesus, Corinth, Philippi, and Thessalonica. He traveled by land and sea, enduring hardships, persecution, and opposition, all because he believed that everyone, everywhere, deserved to hear the gospel of Jesus Christ.

Paul's willingness to pioneer new ways of spreading the gospel was driven by his deep conviction that Jesus was the only way to salvation. He knew that without hearing the message of Christ, people would remain lost in their sins. That conviction gave him the courage to keep pushing the boundaries of where the gospel had been preached. He wasn't content to stay in places where the message was already known; instead, he continually sought out new people, new cities, and new regions to share the gospel. Paul's pioneering spirit wasn't just about geographic expansion—it was about reaching hearts that the love of Christ had never touched. He didn't see barriers, whether they were cultural, linguistic, or religious. He only saw opportunities to share the good news with those most needed it.

One of the most remarkable aspects of Paul's pioneering ministry was his adaptability. Paul understood that sharing the gospel required different approaches depending on the people he was trying to reach. When he preached to Jews, he used the Scriptures to show them that Jesus was the fulfillment of the Old Testament prophecies. When he preached to Gentiles, he used reasoning and examples from their culture to point them to Christ. Paul's willingness to adapt his methods while staying true to the message of the gospel is a powerful example for us today. He was innovative, creative, and bold in finding new ways to communicate the truth of Jesus to people who had never heard it before. Paul's pioneering spirit teaches us that we must be open to new ways of sharing the gospel, always seeking to meet people where they are and speak in ways they can understand.

Even in his final years, when Paul was imprisoned in Rome, he didn't stop pioneering. He continued to preach the kingdom of God and teach about Jesus, even though his circumstances were limited. Paul's imprisonment didn't silence him; it became another platform for him to share the gospel. He wrote letters to the churches he had established, encouraging, teaching, and continuing to guide them in their faith. These letters, which we now know as the Pauline Epistles, have become a foundational part of the New Testament and continue impacting believers worldwide. Paul's pioneering spirit transcended his physical limitations. Even though he was in chains, his message was not. He found new ways to reach people with the gospel, showing us that no matter our circumstances, there is always a way to share the message of Jesus.

Paul's pioneering spirit also extended to his relationships. He didn't just preach to large crowds; he invested in individuals, raising the next generation of leaders who would carry on the mission after he was gone. Paul mentored and discipled people like Timothy, Titus, and Silas, pouring into their lives and equipping them to continue pioneering the gospel's spread. He knew the mission was more significant than himself, and he intentionally empowered others to step into leadership and take the gospel to new places. Paul's example reminds us that pioneering for the gospel isn't just about doing the work ourselves; it's about raising others to join us in the mission. We are called to invest in the lives of others, to disciple and mentor them so that together, we can reach more people for Christ than we ever could alone.

Paul's pioneering spirit was also marked by perseverance. He faced incredible challenges and opposition throughout his ministry but never gave up. He was beaten, stoned, shipwrecked, and imprisoned, yet he continued to press on, always looking for the next opportunity to share the gospel. Paul's resilience in the face of hardship is a testament to his unwavering faith and belief that the gospel was worth any sacrifice. He knew that pioneering new ground for the Kingdom of God would not be easy, but he was willing to endure whatever came his way because he believed that the message of Jesus was worth it. Paul's perseverance challenges us to keep pushing forward in our efforts to share the gospel, even when the road is complex and the obstacles seem insurmountable.

Paul's pioneering ministry also shows us the importance of relying on the Holy Spirit. Paul didn't embark on his mission in his strength; he was led by the Spirit every step of the way. The Holy Spirit guided, opened doors for him, and empowered him to speak boldly and effectively. Paul knew that pioneering for the gospel was not something he could do alone; he needed the power of the Spirit to accomplish the work God had called him to. This is a reminder for all of us that we, too, must rely on the Holy Spirit as we seek to pioneer new ways of sharing the gospel. The mission is too big, and the challenges are too significant for us to do it on our strength. But with the Holy Spirit guiding and empowering us, there is no limit to what we can accomplish for the Kingdom of God.

Paul's pioneering efforts weren't just about his ministry but about laying a foundation for the future. He knew that his work would have a lasting impact long after he was gone. Paul planted seeds of faith in people and places that would continue to grow and bear fruit for generations. His letters, teachings, and the churches he established have shaped Christian history. Paul's willingness to pioneer new ground for the gospel reminds us that our work for Christ has eternal significance. When we step out in faith to share the gospel and pioneer new ways of reaching people, we participate in something far more significant than ourselves. We are building the Kingdom of God, and the impact of our efforts will continue long after we are gone.

In conclusion, Paul's life is a powerful example of what it means to be a pioneer for the gospel. From the beginning of his ministry to the very end, Paul was constantly breaking new ground, reaching new people, and finding new ways to share the message of Jesus. His pioneering spirit was marked by creativity, adaptability, perseverance, and a deep reliance on the Holy Spirit. Paul's willingness to go where no one else had gone and to do whatever it took to spread the gospel challenges us to be bold in our efforts to reach the lost. We are called to be pioneers for Christ, always looking for new ways to share the good news and reach people who have never heard it. Like Paul, we must be willing to push past our comfort zones, take risks, and trust that God will guide us and empower us as we seek to build His Kingdom. The work of spreading the gospel is far from finished, and there are still many places and people who need to hear the message of Jesus. Let us follow Paul's example and embrace the call to be pioneers for the gospel, knowing that our efforts will have an eternal impact and that we are part of something far more significant than ourselves.

Chapter 12 - Perpetual Faithfulness

Paul's life was the ultimate story of perpetual faithfulness—a steadfast commitment to proclaiming the gospel of Jesus Christ with boldness and confidence from the moment of his conversion until the end of his ministry. In Acts 28:31, we find Paul under house arrest in Rome, preaching "with all confidence, no man forbidding him." Even in chains, Paul was still proclaiming Christ with the same fire and boldness he had when he first began. His situation may have changed, but his message and faithfulness to God's calling on his life never wavered. From the Damascus road to his Roman imprisonment, Paul's life testified to the power of faithfulness—faithfulness to the gospel, the mission of spreading the name of Jesus, and the God who had transformed his heart. His faithfulness was not a flash in the pan or a burst of enthusiasm that faded over time. A deep, abiding, and persistent commitment to Christ carried him through every trial, hardship, and obstacle he faced.

Paul's journey as a follower of Christ began with a dramatic and life-changing encounter with Jesus on the road to Damascus. In an instant, his life was turned upside down. Once a persecutor of Christians, Paul became one of the most passionate and determined preachers of the gospel. But what made Paul's ministry remarkable was how he started and finished. Paul didn't just burn brightly for a season and then fade away. He didn't allow the pressures, persecutions, or imprisonments he faced to dim his passion for Christ. Instead, he remained faithful to his mission, even as the years passed and the challenges multiplied. Circumstances or external rewards did not drive his unwavering commitment to preaching the gospel. Still, by a deep, internal conviction that Jesus was the Messiah, the Savior of the world, and that sharing that message was the most important thing he could ever do.

Throughout his ministry, Paul faced countless trials. He was beaten, stoned, shipwrecked, imprisoned, and constantly persecuted for his faith. Yet, none of these things could shake his confidence in Christ or his determination to continue preaching the gospel. Paul understood that faithfulness to the gospel wasn't about how easy or comfortable life was—it was about staying the course, even when the road was hard. He knew that the message of Jesus was too important to be silenced by fear, suffering, or opposition. And so, he pressed on, preaching in synagogues, public squares, homes, and even prisons. He never lost sight of God's mission, and that mission fueled his faithfulness to the very end. Paul's life is a powerful example of what it means to endure in faith, keep going even when everything around you is falling apart, and stay faithful to God's calling, no matter the cost.

Paul's faithfulness was rooted in his deep, unshakable confidence in Christ. He knew that Jesus was the Son of God, the Savior who had come to rescue humanity from sin and death. This was not just head knowledge for Paul—it was the very foundation of his life. He had experienced the transforming power of Christ firsthand, and that experience gave him the strength and courage to remain faithful, no matter what trials he faced. Paul's confidence in the gospel was unshakable because it was grounded in the truth of who Jesus is. He knew that his message was not just another religious philosophy—it was the truth that could set people free. And so, even when he was under house arrest in Rome, with his freedom stripped away, Paul continued to preach with boldness and confidence. He knew the gospel could not be chained, even if he was. His faithfulness to the message of Christ transcended his circumstances because his confidence was in God, not in his abilities or situation.

Paul's faithfulness was not just about preaching the gospel but about living it out daily. He didn't just talk about Jesus; he lived like Jesus. His life was a reflection of the message he preached. Paul was faithful not only in his words but in his actions. He loved others, served selflessly, and endured hardship with grace and humility. He poured himself out for the sake of the gospel, putting others' needs above his own and always pointing people to Jesus. Paul's faithfulness wasn't just about his public ministry but his private devotion to Christ. He was a man of prayer, constantly seeking God's guidance and strength. His faithfulness flowed from his deep relationship with Christ, a relationship that sustained him through every trial and empowered him to finish his race well.

One of the most potent aspects of Paul's faithfulness was his ability to finish strong. Many start well but struggle to maintain their commitment over the long haul. But Paul was different. He completed his race with the same passion, boldness, and confidence he had when he started. Even as he faced the reality of his death, Paul's focus remained on Christ. He wasn't consumed with fear or regret but with the desire to see the gospel continue to spread. Paul knew that his time on earth was ending, but he also knew that the mission of spreading the gospel was far from finished. And so, even in his final days, he continued to preach, write letters, encourage believers, and proclaim the name of Jesus. His faithfulness to the end is a powerful reminder that the Christian life is not a sprint—it's a marathon. And like Paul, we are called to run with endurance, to stay faithful to Christ, and to finish our race well.

Paul's faithfulness challenges us to examine our own lives. Are we staying faithful to the message of the gospel, even when it's hard? Are we remaining confident in Christ, even when we face opposition, hardship, or uncertainty? Like Paul, we are called to finish our race with the same faithfulness and confidence with which we started. It's easy to be passionate about Christ initially when everything is new and exciting. But steadfast faithfulness is measured over the long haul. It's about staying committed to Christ through every season of life—through the joys, struggles, triumphs, and trials. It's about continuing to preach the gospel, even when no one seems to be listening. It's about remaining confident in Christ, even when the world is falling apart. Paul's life reminds us that faithfulness is not about how we start but how we finish. And we are called to finish strong, just as Paul did.

Paul's faithfulness also reminds us that we are not in this race alone. Just as Paul relied on the support and prayers of fellow believers, we, too, need the encouragement of others to stay faithful. The Christian life is not meant to be lived in isolation. We are part of the body of Christ, and we need each other to stay strong and finish well. Paul was constantly surrounded by fellow believers who encouraged him, prayed for him, and partnered with him in the mission of spreading the gospel. His faithfulness was not just a result of his strength—it was a result of the strength he found in the community. This is a powerful reminder that we, too, need the support of our brothers and sisters in Christ to stay faithful to the end. We are called to encourage one another, to lift each other in prayer, and to run this race together.

In conclusion, Paul's life is a powerful example of perpetual faithfulness that endured to the end. From his conversion to his final days under house arrest,

Paul remained bold and confident in his proclamation of the gospel. Even in the face of persecution, hardship, and imprisonment, his unwavering commitment to Christ is a testimony to the power of faith and the strength of a deep relationship with Jesus. Paul's life challenges us to remain faithful to the message of the gospel, no matter what trials we face. We are called to finish our race with the same faithfulness and confidence we had when we first began, trusting that God will give us the strength to endure. Like Paul, let us stay the course, remain bold in our proclamation of Christ, and finish strong, knowing that our faithfulness will have an eternal impact on the Kingdom of God.

These lessons reflect Paul's consistency, boldness, and unwavering commitment to the message of Christ throughout his life. Like Paul, we are called to be faithful and purposeful in our gospel proclamation.

Conclusion

As we conclude "The Kingdom Builder: Paul's Bold Proclamation of Christ," we are left with a mighty challenge. Paul's life is a shining example of what it means to live utterly devoted to Christ, no matter the cost. Throughout his incredible journey, Paul showed us what it looks like to be bold, faithful, and unrelenting in spreading the gospel. His story is not just one of a man transformed by the love of Jesus but a call to every Christian to follow in his footsteps. Paul was not extraordinary because of his background, talents, or education—he was remarkable because of his unwavering commitment to the gospel and his willingness to lay everything on the line for the sake of Christ. The lessons we learn from Paul's life are not just for admiration; they are meant to stir our hearts to action. As believers, we are called to carry on the work that Paul began, continuing to build the Kingdom of God with the same passion, boldness, and faithfulness that defined his life.

Paul's life teaches us that living for Christ is not a passive or comfortable calling—it requires sacrifice, perseverance, and a deep reliance on God's strength. In a world that often resists the gospel's message, we must be bold like Paul, unafraid to speak the truth, and stand up for our faith, even when it's unpopular or dangerous. Paul's boldness wasn't about being loud or confrontational; it was about being unashamed of the gospel, knowing that it was the power of God for salvation. Today, Christians are called to speak boldly about Jesus in a world that desperately needs to hear the truth. Whether in our workplaces, schools, communities, or homes, we must not be afraid to share the message of hope and salvation that we have been entrusted with. Paul's example challenges us to stop waiting for the perfect moment or ideal circumstances and to proclaim Christ with boldness in every opportunity we are given.

But boldness alone is not enough. Paul's life was also marked by deep perseverance. He faced countless trials, including beatings, imprisonments, shipwrecks, and constant opposition, yet he never wavered in his commitment to the gospel. Paul understood that following Christ meant enduring hardship, and he embraced it with joy because he knew that his sufferings were nothing compared to the glory that awaited him in eternity. This is a lesson we must take to heart. As followers of Christ, we will face challenges—sometimes even persecution—for our faith. But like Paul, we are called to press on, trusting that God will give us the strength to endure. Our faithfulness in the face of trials is a powerful testimony to the world of the truth and worth of the gospel. We must remain steadfast, knowing our perseverance will bear fruit for the Kingdom of God.

One of the most profound lessons we can learn from Paul's life is the importance of finishing well. Paul didn't just start his race with passion—he finished strong. Even in his final days, while under house arrest in Rome, Paul continued to preach and teach with the same zeal and confidence that had characterized his entire ministry. He never allowed his circumstances to dampen his faith or diminish his commitment to Christ. This is a powerful reminder that our faith journey is not about short bursts of enthusiasm but about enduring faithfulness over the long haul. We are called to run the race with endurance, keeping our eyes fixed on Jesus and finishing strong, no matter our challenges. Paul's life shows us that it's not how we start that matters most—it's how we finish. Will we remain faithful to the end, continuing to serve Christ with passion and perseverance, even in the face of hardship or uncertainty?

As we reflect on the lessons from "The Kingdom Builder," it's clear that Paul's life was not just about building churches or spreading a message—it was about building the Kingdom of God. He understood that his mission was far more significant than himself and was willing to sacrifice everything to see God's Kingdom advance. This is the heart of the Christian life: we are called to be Kingdom builders. Whether we are called to preach, serve, give, or share the gospel in our everyday lives, we are all part of God's mission to bring the message of Jesus to the world. The lessons we've learned from Paul's life should inspire us to live with the same sense of purpose and urgency. There is no greater mission than building God's Kingdom, and each of us has a role. Like Paul, we must be willing to lay down our desires, comforts, and fears for the sake of Christ and His gospel.

The challenge for every Christian is to take the lessons from Paul's life and apply them to our own. We are called to be bold in proclaiming Christ, to persevere through trials, and to remain faithful to the very end. Paul's life was not easy but full of purpose, joy, and eternal impact. As we close this book, we must ask ourselves: Are we willing to live with the same boldness, faithfulness, and perseverance that Paul displayed? Are we willing to be Kingdom builders, fully committed to the mission of Christ, no matter the cost? The world needs more believers like Paul—people who are unashamed of the gospel, willing to go wherever God calls, and determined to finish their race well. Let Paul's life inspire and challenge you to step out in faith, to live boldly for Christ, and to dedicate your life to building His Kingdom. Your journey may not look exactly like Paul's, but the calling is the same: to proclaim Christ, to persevere, and to finish well. The race is set before us—let us run with endurance, knowing that our efforts for the Kingdom will have an eternal impact.

Don't miss out!

Visit the website below and you can sign up to receive emails whenever Joshua Rhoades publishes a new book. There's no charge and no obligation.

https://books2read.com/r/B-A-AJLBB-IINCF

Did you love *The Kingdom Builder Paul's Bold Proclamation of Christ*? Then you should read *Answer The Call - 31 Days of Biblical Action*[1] by Joshua Rhoades!

[2]

"Answer the Call – 31 Days of Biblical Action" is a transformative devotional that challenges you to not only read the Word of God but to live it every day. This powerful 31-day guide is uniquely centered around individual action verbs drawn from Scripture, calling you to apply specific actions in your daily life. Each day highlights a verb—such as love, serve, forgive, trust, or pray—and encourages you to engage deeply with its biblical meaning while putting it into practice.

This is not just a devotional for reflection; it's a call to action, a stirring reminder that faith is most alive when it moves. By focusing on one verb each day, "Answer the Call" helps you to integrate the teachings of the Bible into your daily routine, bringing the message of Scripture to life in practical and meaningful ways.

The book invites you to engage your heart and hands as you follow Christ's example. Each action verb acts as a catalyst for spiritual growth, reminding you

---

1. https://books2read.com/u/4X5kG9

2. https://books2read.com/u/4X5kG9

that faith isn't static but dynamic and responsive. Whether it's through acts of kindness, moments of prayer, or stepping out in faith, these daily challenges will inspire you to live out your beliefs with boldness and purpose.

By the end of the 31 days, you will feel encouraged, empowered, and renewed. "Answer the Call" will leave you transformed, ready to live your faith in real, actionable ways, embodying the teachings of Scripture in every area of your life.